Never give in, never give
never; never; never; never
in nothing, great or small,
large or petty – never give in except
to convictions of honour
and good sense.
Never yield to force.
Never yield to the apparently
overwhelming might of the enemy.

SIR WINSTON CHURCHILL

Risk more than others think is safe.
Care more than others think is wise.
Dream more than others think is practical.
Expect more than others think is possible.

CLAUDE BISSELL

JULY 2

If in doubt, all you ever
need to ask yourself
is this "Is this the kindest
thing to do?" And that
question will provide you
with all the answers
you'll ever need.

SIÂN E. MORGAN

Bᴇ ʙʀᴀᴠᴇ,
ᴛᴀᴋᴇ ʀɪꜱᴋꜱ.
ɴᴏᴛʜɪɴɢ ᴄᴀɴ
ꜱᴜʙꜱᴛɪᴛᴜᴛᴇ
ᴇxᴘᴇʀɪᴇɴᴄᴇ.

PAULO COELHO

I would be true, for there are those who trust me;
I would be pure, for there are those who care;
I would be strong, for there is much to suffer;
I would be brave, for there is much to dare.
I would be friend of all – the foe, the friendless;
I would be giving and forget the gift;
I would be humble, for I know my weakness;
I would look up – and laugh – and love – and lift.

HOWARD ARNOLD WALTER

JULY **5**

Courage is finding the inner strength and bravery
required when confronting danger, difficulty or opposition.
Courage is the energy current behind all great actions
and the spark that ignites the initial baby steps of growth.
It resides deep within each of us, ready to be accessed in those
moments when you need to forge ahead or break through
seemingly insurmountable barriers.

CHERIE CARTER-SCOTT

I'd rather be an optimist and a fool, than a pessimist and right.

ALBERT EINSTEIN

Never say
"I cannot face this."
You can.
And you can endure
and succeed.
Believe in yourself.
You are stronger
than you realise.

HANNAH C. KLEIN

One ought never to turn one's back on a threatened danger and try to run away from it. If you do that, you will double the danger. But if you meet it promptly and without flinching, you will reduce the danger by half.

SIR WINSTON CHURCHILL

A JOURNEY OF A THOUSAND MILES BEGINS WITH A SINGLE STEP.

LAO TZU

When we have hope, we discover powers within ourselves we may have never known – the power to make sacrifices, to endure, to heal, and to love. Once we choose hope, everything is possible. We are all on this sea together. But the lighthouse is always there, ready to show us the way home.

CHRISTOPHER REEVE

JULY 8

People are like stained
glass windows;
they sparkle and shine
when the sun is out, but it's when
the darkness sets in that their
true beauty is revealed only if there
is light from within.

DR. ELISABETH KUBLER-ROSS

The world breaks
everyone,
and afterward
many are strong
in the broken places.

ERNEST HEMINGWAY

Breathe. Let go.
And remind yourself
that this very moment
is the only one
you know
you have for sure.

OPRAH WINFREY

Learn from
yesterday,
live for today,
hope for tomorrow.
The important thing
is not to stop
questioning.

ALBERT EINSTEIN

You have a choice. You can gripe about what people are doing, or you can go out and get involved and work your tail off and change what they're doing. I much prefer the second alternative. You feel better at the end, win or lose.

PATTY MURRAY

JUNE **25**

MAKE EACH DAY YOUR MASTERPIECE.

JOHN WOODEN

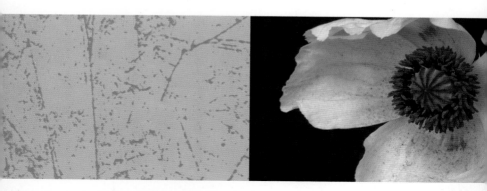

Whatever else, be decent.
You don't have to be perfect.
You don't have to be brilliant,
just do the right thing.
If you say you are
going to do something,
you have to do it.

BILL BRYSON

When we least expect it,
life sets us a challenge to
test our courage and willingness
to change. At such a moment,
there is no point in pretending
that nothing has happened or
in saying that we are not yet ready.
The challenge will not wait.
Life does not look back.

PAULO COELHO

If you decide
on climbing a mountain
you must expect a few bruises.
Sharpen your skills.
Check your gear.
Summon your courage.
Watch the weather and begin
the ascent.
In the Alps. In life.

ODILE DORMEUIL

Laughing cheerfulness
throws sunlight
on all the paths of life.

JEAN PAUL RICHTER

Praise and blame,
gain and loss,
pleasure and sorrow
come and go
like the wind.
To be happy, rest like
a great tree in the
midst of them all.

GAUTAMA BUDDHA

We must constantly build
dykes of courage to hold back
the flood of fear.

MARTIN LUTHER KING JR.

JULY **14**

Wisdom can come to those who unravel all the laws
of space and time, who create wonders in art
and dance and music, who find ways to heal the body
and the mind, who attempt to guide the nations...
and to those quiet souls who seem to live most ordinary lives,
known only as people comforting and kind –
good workers and good friends.

PAM BROWN

HOWEVER LONG THE NIGHT, THE DAWN WILL BREAK.

AFRICAN PROVERB

THE BRAVEST ARE THOSE WHO ARE MOST AFRAID, BUT THAT ENDURE.

PAMELA DUGDALE

JUNE **20**

If it is not truthful and not helpful, don't say it.
If it is truthful and not helpful, don't say it.
If it is not truthful and helpful, don't say it.
If it is truthful and helpful, wait for the right time.

GAUTAMA BUDDHA

JULY **16**

Be brave
today.
The darkest
night
will pass.

SARAH KNOWLES BOLTON

Never forget,
TODAY,
YOU HAVE 100%
OF YOUR LIFE LEFT.

TOM HOPKINS

Yes is the most powerful word.
Yes is freeing and inspiring.
It means permission. It means possibility.
It means you give yourself and others the chance to dream.
Saying Yes makes you feel good.

HOWARD BEHAR

JUNE **18**

To struggle when
hope is banished!
To live when
life's salt is gone!
To dwell in a dream
that's vanished –
To ensure,
and go calmly on!

BEN JOHNSON

THE FUTURE
BELONGS TO THOSE
WHO BELIEVE
IN THE BEAUTY
OF THEIR DREAMS.

ELEANOR ROOSEVELT

JULY **19**

Fear is not your enemy.
It is a compass
pointing you
to the areas where
you need to grow.

STEVE PAVLINA

All people
who have achieved
great things
have been dreamers.

ORISON SWETT MARDEN

Compassion unites us and helps us
to discover one another and ourselves.
It does not cancel out suffering or evil but
it offers us a way of combating it. And this way of living
enriches each of us, quietly, as a gentle shower
before dawn gives life to the tired soil and the thirsty bush.

SUE RYDER

Courage
IS A QUIETNESS...
BORN OF
FACING UP TO LIFE.

EMILY SARGENT COUNCILMAN

It is not the strongest
of the species that survive,
nor the most intelligent,
but the one most
responsive to change.

CHARLES DARWIN

I ASK NOT FOR A LIGHTER BURDEN,
BUT FOR BROADER SHOULDERS.

YIDDISH PROVERB

...forget pursuing happiness.
Pin your hopes on work, on family, on learning,
on knowing, on loving.
Forget pursuing happiness; pursue
these other things and happiness will come.

WILLIAM J. BENNETT

JULY **22**

Go with the pain, let it take you...
Open your palms and your body
to the pain. It comes in waves like a tide,
and you must be open as a vessel lying
on the beach, letting it fill you up and then,
retreating, leaving you empty and clear...
With a deep breath – it has to be as deep
as the pain – one reaches a kind of inner
freedom from pain, as though the pain
were not yours but your body's.

ANNE MORROW LINDBERGH

In our moments
of anguish, gates barred
for ever seem
to open and let in many
a flood of light.

SWAMI VIVEKANANDA

Security is mostly a superstition.
It does not exist in nature, nor do
the children of men as a whole experience it.
Avoiding danger is no safer in the long run
than outright exposure. Life is either
a daring adventure, or nothing.

HELEN KELLER
(BORN BOTH DEAF AND BLIND)

JUNE **12**

"This too will pass." I was taught these words by my grandmother as a phrase that is to be used at all times in your life. When things are spectacularly dreadful; when things are absolutely appalling; when everything is superb and wonderful and marvellous and happy – say these four words to yourself. They will give you a sense of perspective and help you also to make the most of what is good and be stoical about what is bad.

CLAIRE RAYNER

Watch your thoughts; they become words.
Watch your words; they become actions.
Watch your actions; they become habits.
Watch your habits; they become character.
Watch your character; it becomes your destiny.

LAO TZU

Stop acting as if life
is a rehearsal.
Live this day as if it
were your last.
The past is over and gone.
The future
is not guaranteed.

DR. WAYNE W. DYER

I knew that if I failed
I wouldn't regret that,
but I knew the one thing
I might regret
is not trying.

JEFF BEZOS

The blessing I wish
each child is courage.
The courage to work towards a goal
even under great difficulties.
The courage to accept
criticism or rejection.
The courage to pick themselves
up when they have fallen –
and go on with better
understanding and a high heart.

PAM BROWN

Courage doesn't always roar.
Sometimes courage is the quiet voice
at the end of the day that says
"I will try again tomorrow."

MARY ANNE RADMACHER

Hope begins in the dark,
the stubborn hope
that if you just show up
and try to do the right thing,
the dawn will come.
You wait and watch and work:
you don't give up.

ANNE LAMOTT

Always bear in mind
that your own resolution to succeed
is more important
than any other one thing.

ABRAHAM LINCOLN

JUNE **8**

My will shall shape my future. Whether I fail or succeed shall be no one's doing but my own. I am the force; I can clear any obstacle before me or I can be lost in the maze. My choice; my responsibility; win or lose, only I hold the key to my destiny.

ELAINE MAXWELL

We should
never be so busy
that we miss out
on the sheer
wonder
of being alive.

EMILY DICKINSON

You're winning. You simply cannot fail.
The only obstacle is doubt... Don't think defeat, don't talk
defeat, the word will rob you of your strength.

MINNIE AUMONIER

IF YOU CAN DREAM IT, THEN YOU CAN ACHIEVE IT.

ZIG ZIGLAR

Hope is being
able to see
that there is light
despite all the
darkness.

ARCHBISHOP DESMOND TUTU

I should never have made my success in life
if I had not bestowed upon
the least thing I have ever undertaken,
the same attention and care
that I have bestowed upon the greatest.

CHARLES DICKENS

JUNE 5

KEEP YOUR FEARS TO YOURSELF, BUT SHARE YOUR COURAGE WITH OTHERS.

ROBERT LOUIS STEVENSON

JULY **31**

The greatest gift in life
is the ability
to think great thoughts
and have the strength
to take action
so that those thoughts
become reality
in this wonderful
and abundant world.

JACK BLACK

Make the most of
yourself by fanning
the tiny, inner sparks
of possibility into
flames of achievement.

GOLDA MEIR

I found that I could find the energy…
that I could find the determination to keep on going.
I learned that your mind can amaze your body,
if you just keep telling yourself,
I can do it… I can do it… I can do it!

JON ERICKSON

JUNE **3**

To be brave is not
to be immune to suffering.
It is to hold onto hope,
and to endure as best we can.

PAM BROWN

AUGUST **2**

EVEN AFTER A BAD HARVEST THERE MUST BE A SOWING.

SENECA THE YOUNGER

JUNE **2**

Sometimes
the smallest step
in the right direction
ends up being
the biggest step
of your life.

EMMA STONE

WHEN YOU
CEASE
TO DREAM
YOU CEASE
TO LIVE.

MALCOLM S. FORBES

Bravery does not mean
you are without fear.
It means you have the courage
to face your fear.

RAMA VERNON

More smiling,
less worrying.
More compassion,
less judgment.
More blessed,
less stressed.
More love, less hate.

ROY T. BENNETT

HOPE HAS TO BE FOUND: A BRIGHTNESS IN ANYONE'S DARK.

BARNEY BARDSLEY

The truly courageous go about
helping others
with a hopeful heart,
against all odds.

PAM BROWN

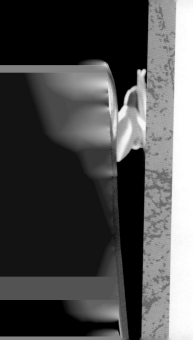

Set fire
to the broken
pieces;
start anew.

LAUREN DESTEFANO

Allow hope
to penetrate your
darkness
and it will give you
comfort.
And strength.
And patience.

PAMELA DUGDALE

It is important to stay close enough
to the pulse of life to feel its rhythm,
to be comforted by its steadiness, to know
that life is vital, and one's own minute living
a torn fragment of the larger cloth.

MARJORIE KINNAN RAWLINGS

AUGUST 7

EVERY DAY
HAS AN
ASTOUNDING GIFT.
OPEN EACH
EAGERLY.

PAM BROWN

Out of suffering have emerged
the strongest souls, the most massive
characters are seamed with scars...

EDWIN HUBBEL CHAPIN

AUGUST 8

Love the moment. Flowers grow out of dark moments.
Therefore, each moment is vital.
It affects the whole. Life is a succession of such moments
and to live each, is to succeed.

CORITA KENT

MAY **27**

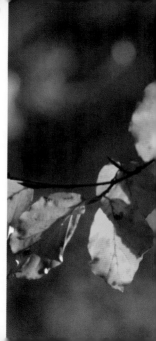

THE ONLY
WAY OUT
IS THROUGH.

HELEN KELLER
(BORN BOTH DEAF AND BLIND)

If your life is built on
something solid, the winds
and the storms of life may blow,
you may sway back and forth,
but you will stand strong
as long as you firmly
hold on to that life-giving force.

BEAR HEART (MUSKOGEE)

People are always blaming their circumstances
for what they are. I don't believe in circumstances.
The people who get on in this world are the people
who get up and look for the circumstances they want, and,
if they can't find them, they make them.

GEORGE BERNARD SHAW

Expose yourself to your deepest fear; after that the fear of freedom shrinks and vanishes. You are free.

JIM MORRISON

MAY **25**

Hope is what encourages us
to keep on living,
learning and loving.
Hope will never abandon us
when life is unexpectedly filled
with things which sadden
and disappoint.
Hope will get us through
the truly rough times.

AUTHOR UNKNOWN

Men and women
are limited
not by the place
of their birth,
not by the colour
of their skin,
but by the size
of their hope.

JOHN JOHNSON

I never used to understand what fearlessness was. I thought that some lucky people were just born unafraid, and that was why they could surf huge waves and climb massive overhanging cliffs with no ropes. But real fearlessness has got nothing to do with being unafraid. It's about doing things anyway, getting on with it, living, whether you're afraid or not.

CATRINA DAVIS

AUGUST **12**

Have courage
for the great sorrows of life
and patience
for the small ones
and when you have finished
your daily task,
go to sleep in peace.

VICTOR HUGO

Our greatest glory
is not in never falling,
but in rising
every time we fall.

CONFUCIUS

Enjoy the blessings of the day…
and the evils bear patiently;
for this day only is ours: we are dead to yesterday,
and not born to tomorrow.

JEREMY TAYLOR

MAY **22**

The power to live a full, adult, living, breathing life in close contact with that I love – the earth and the wonders thereof, the sea, the sun… I want to enter into it, to be part of it, to live in it, to learn from it, to lose all that is superficial and acquired in me, and to become a conscious direct human being. I want, by understanding myself, to understand others. I want to be all that I am capable of becoming…

KATHERINE MANSFIELD

You should nurse
your dreams
and protect them
through bad times
and tough times
to the sunshine and light
which always come.

THOMAS WOODROW WILSON

When the world says,
"give up"
hope whispers,
"try it one more time."

AUTHOR UNKNOWN

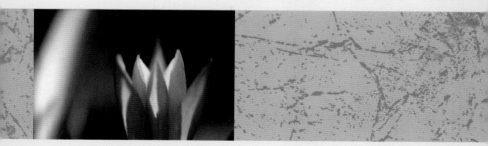

Did I offer peace today?
Did I bring a smile to someone's face?
Did I say words of healing?
Did I let go of my anger
and resentment? Did I forgive?
Did I love? These are the real questions.
I must trust that the little bit of love
that I sow now will bear many fruits.

HENRI J. NOUWEN

The secret to change
is to focus all
of your energy, not on
fighting the old,
but on building the new.

SOCRATES

There are but two roads that lead to an important goal and to the doing of great things: strength and perseverance. Strength is the lot of but a few privileged people, but austere perseverance, harsh and continuous, may be employed by the smallest of us and rarely fails of its purpose, for its silent power grows irresistibly greater with time.

JOHANN WOLFGANG VON GOETHE

MAY **19**

You are never alone.
You are part of
the Family of Man.
And you matter.

ODILE DORMEUIL

A strong
positive mental
attitude
will create more
miracles than
any wonder drug.

PATRICIA NEAL

One word frees us
from all the weight and pain in life.
That word is love.

SOPHOCLES

AUGUST **18**

It's going to be okay.
No matter
how hard your
rock bottom is,
you can rise above it
and you can come back.

DEMI LOVATO

All our dreams
can come true –
if we have
the courage to
pursue them.

WALT DISNEY

The highest point
a person can attain
is not Knowledge, or Virtue,
or Goodness, or Victory,
but something even greater,
more heroic,
and more despairing:
Sacred Awe!

NIKOS KAZANTZAKIS

AUGUST **20**

WHEN WE ARE FLAT
ON OUR BACKS
THERE IS NO WAY TO LOOK
BUT UP.

ROGER BABSON

CHARACTER IS MADE OF DUTY
AND LOVE AND SYMPATHY,
AND, ABOVE ALL,
OF LIVING AND WORKING FOR OTHERS.

ROBERT GREEN INGERSOLL

MAY **15**

There is beauty around us,
in things large and small,
in friends, family, the
countryside, a singing bird.
Stop to reflect, to give thanks,
to contemplate the gift
of another day.
Touch the wonders of life
and rejoice.

ANTON CHEKHOV

Because we understand
the value of money,
we take care not to waste it.
If we valued time, energy
and positive thoughts,
we would likewise economise.
The result would be
a life full of
meaning and purpose.

DADI JANKI

We should never give up on
our hopes and dreams.
The path may be rocky and
twisted, but the world is
waiting for that special contribution
each of us was born to make.
What it takes is the courage to
follow those whispers of wisdom
that guide us from inside.

MARILYN JOHNSON KONDWANI

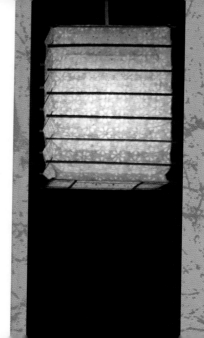

The main thing is
having a positive approach to life,
doing things that you want to do,
and being happy about
what you're doing.
If something is awful,
think how to make it better
and never feel defeated
and give up, because thinking
positively can eventually
turn things around.

JERRY HALL

Bravery is believing in yourself, and that thing nobody can teach you.

EL CORDOBES

AUGUST 23

Believe in yourself!
Have faith in
your abilities!
Without a humble
but reasonable confidence
in your own powers,
you cannot be
successful or happy.

NORMAN VINCENT PEALE

Every great dream begins
with a dreamer. Always remember,
you have within you
the strength, the patience,
and the passion to reach
for the stars to change the world.

HARRIET TUBMAN

Courage is about learning how to function despite
the fear; to put aside your instincts to run
or give in completely to the anger born from fear.
Courage is about using your brain and your heart when
every cell of your body is screaming at you to fight or flee –
and then following through on
what you believe is the right thing to do.

JIM BUTCHER

Make it a rule of life
never to regret
and never look back.
Regret is an appalling
waste of energy;
you can't build on it;
it is good only for wallowing in.

KATHERINE MANSFIELD

...strength and courage aren't always measured in medals and victories. They are measured in the struggles we overcome. The strongest people are not always the people who win, but the people who don't give up when they lose.

ASHLEY HODGESON

MAY **10**

I thought,
"Why doesn't someone
do something about this?"
And then I realised
I am someone.

AUTHOR UNKNOWN

A failure that we learn from
is not a failure at all.

FR BRIAN D'ARCY

Failing will be part of your adventure.

VICTOR KIAM

MAY 9

Courage takes many forms. There is physical courage, there is moral courage. Then there is a still higher type of courage – the courage to brave pain, to live with it, to never let others know of it and to still find joy in life; to wake up in the morning with an enthusiasm for the day ahead.

HOWARD COSELL

AUGUST **27**

To TRAVEL
HOPEFULLY
IS A BETTER
THING THAN
TO ARRIVE.

ROBERT LOUIS STEVENSON

Go confidently in
the direction of your dreams!
Live the life you've imagined.
As you simplify your life,
the laws of the universe
will be simpler; solitude
will not be solitude,
poverty will not be poverty,
nor weakness weakness.

HENRY DAVID THOREAU

Don't be too busy, too serious,
too sensible – at least,
not all the time!
Remember to have a little fun,
enjoy a little nonsense, a sprinkling
of dreams, even a few daydreams,
to balance life's doing.
Make the most, too, of life's
small joys and pleasures as well
as its great happinesses.
It will help you to cope all the better
with the ups and down of life!

FROM "THE FRIENDSHIP BOOK OF FRANCIS GAY"

What really matters is the will to meet with courage the difficulties of life.

HELEN KELLER
(BORN BOTH DEAF AND BLIND)

AUGUST **29**

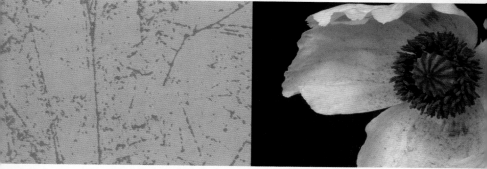

THE GREATEST GIFT
YOU CAN GIVE
IS THE GIFT
OF YOURSELF;
IT IS A HUGE GIFT.

JOHN O'DONOHUE

FACING IT –
ALWAYS FACING IT –
THAT'S THE
WAY TO GET THROUGH.
FACE IT!

JOSEPH CONRAD

Everyone has inside them a piece of good news!
The good news is that you
really don't know how great you can be,
how much you can love, what you can accomplish,
and what your potential is!

ANNE FRANK

MAY

Be soft. Do not let the world make you hard.
Do not let pain make you hate. Do not let the bitterness
steal your sweetness. Take pride that even though
the rest of the world may disagree,
you still believe it to be a beautiful place.

KURT VONNEGUT

AUGUST **31**

Make someone smile whenever you can,
you never know how much of a difference
you could be making in their life at that moment.

AUTHOR UNKNOWN

MAY **4**

…we all search for happiness,
each and every one of us, but see it
incorrectly, in the wrong things,
which is why so few of us can find
our way out of our own deserts.
Money, power, fame – these are not
the essential goals for happiness.
If anything, focusing on those will
keep you even further from the
realisation of your dreams.

ERIN BROCKOVICH

Life is either
a daring adventure
or nothing.
To keep our faces toward
change and behave like
free spirits
in the presence of fate
is strength undefeatable.

HELEN KELLER
(BORN BOTH DEAF AND BLIND)

Keep a green tree
in our heart
and perhaps a singing
bird will come.

CHINESE PROVERB

In the depth of winter,
I finally learned that within me there
lay an invincible summer.

ALBERT CAMUS

Let yourself be silently drawn
by the strange pull of what you really love.
It will not lead you astray.

JALAL AL-DIN MUHAMMAD RUMI

SEPTEMBER 3

Whatever
you can do or
dream you can,
begin it.
Boldness has
genius, power
and magic in it.

JOHANN WOLFGANG VON GOETHE

YOU CAN'T WAIT
FOR INSPIRATION.
YOU HAVE TO
GO AFTER IT
WITH A CLUB.

JACK LONDON

Remembering that
you are going to die
is the best way I know
to avoid the trap of thinking
you have something to lose.
You are already naked.
There is no reason
not to follow your heart.

STEVE JOBS

Change can be
scary, but
it's through change
that great
things happen.

MICA PARIS

We have been dropped into chaos and nothing is as it was.
We look longingly on life as it used to be and wish
we had a chance to do things over again.
But we don't. Our lives are unalterably changed,
and we will never again be the persons we were before.
We have been carried into a larger realm where
we see what truly is important, and it is our responsibility
to carry that knowledge back into our daily lives.
It is our chance to think life afresh.

KENT NERBURN

You got to walk that lonesome valley,
you got to walk it for yourself.
Nobody can walk it for you,
you got to walk it for yourself.

AUTHOR UNKNOWN

SEPTEMBER **6**

Hope, enthusiasm
and wisdom
are to the mind
as food is to the body.
Everyone needs
daily sustenance.

DADI JANKI

${\rm A}$ction always starts
with one first small step –
and you do not have to
know precisely what
your final goal is
to start down the road.

GEORGETTE MOSBACHER

IF YOUR DREAMS DO NOT SCARE YOU, THEY ARE NOT BIG ENOUGH.

ELLEN JOHNSON SIRLEAF

Whether we have it all or we have nothing, we are all faced with the same obstacles: sadness, loss, illness, dying and death. If we are to strive as human beings to gain more wisdom, more kindness and more compassion, we must have the intention to grow as a lotus and open each petal one by one.

KUTENLA, BUDDHIST MONK

SEPTEMBER **8**

When you have landed
at the bottom of a deep dark hole,
take hold of hope –
however frail it seems –
and start to climb.

PAM BROWN

APRIL **26**

Wʜᴀᴛ ᴄᴏᴜɴᴛs ɪs
ɴᴏᴛ ᴛʜᴇ ᴇɴᴏʀᴍɪᴛʏ
ᴏғ ᴛʜᴇ ᴛᴀsᴋ,
ʙᴜᴛ ᴛʜᴇ sɪᴢᴇ
ᴏғ ᴛʜᴇ ᴄᴏᴜʀᴀɢᴇ.

MATTHIEU RICARD

So many paths, that wind and wind,
While just the art of being kind
Is all the sad world needs.

ELLA WHEELER WILCOX

APRIL **25**

I have accepted fear
as a part of life –
specifically the fear
of change… I have
gone ahead despite
the pounding in the heart
that says; turn back.

ERICA JONG

As an old man, looking back on one's life,
it's one of the things that strikes you
most forcibly – that the only thing
that's taught one anything is suffering.
Not success, not happiness, not anything
like that. The only thing that really teaches one
what life's about – the joy of understanding,
the joy of coming into contact with
that life really signifies – is suffering, affliction.

MALCOLM MUGGERIDGE

Hope helps us stand when sadness threatens to buckle us. Hope restores our energy when circumstances seem to defeat us. Hope glorifies the mundane. Hope gives us the courage to dare to be ourselves and to reveal ourselves to others. To live in hope is to believe in light when it is dark, in beauty when ugliness abounds, in peace when conflict seems to reign.

SUZANNE C. COLE

It had been my
repeated experience
that when you said to life
calmly and firmly
(but very firmly!),
"I trust you; do what you must,"
life had an uncanny
way of responding
to your need.

OLGA ILYIN

The most beautiful people are those who have known defeat, known suffering, known struggle, known loss, and have found their way out of the depths. These persons have an appreciation, a sensitivity, and an understanding of life that fills them with compassion, gentleness, and a deep loving concern. Beautiful people do not just happen.

ELISABETH KÜBLER-ROSS

SEPTEMBER **12**

APRIL **22**

And only when we are
no longer afraid do we
begin to live in every
experience, painful
or joyous;
to live in gratitude for
every moment,
to live abundantly.

DOROTHY THOMPSON

Do one thing every day that scares you.

MARY SCHMICH

M y advice is: go outside,
to the fields, enjoy nature and the sunshine,
go out and try
to recapture happiness...

ANNE FRANK

APRIL **21**

The earth is empty.
The trees, once thick with blossom
stand dead against a bitter sky.
The streams are frozen.
The heart has lost all hope.
But see – along the branches new
buds appear and greenness pushes
through the ground unnoticed.
Spring may be slow –
but will at last return.

PAM BROWN

…fame and fortune only
have true worth
when mixed with other
ingredients – like happiness,
harmony and
balance in your life.

RACHEL ELNAUGH

The most visible creators I know of are those
artists whose medium is life itself.
The ones who express the inexpressible –
without brush, hammer, clay, or guitar. They neither
paint nor sculpt – their medium is being.
Whatever their presence touches has increased life.
They see and don't have to draw.
They are the artists of being alive.

J. STONE

SEPTEMBER 15

HOWEVER LONG
THE NIGHT
MAY LAST,
THERE WILL
BE MORNING.

MOROCCAN PROVERB

Courageous risks
are life-giving,
they help you grow,
make you brave
and better than
you think you are.

JOAN L. CURCIO

You have to count on
living every single day
in a way you believe
will make you feel good
about your life – so that
if it were over tomorrow,
you'd be content
with yourself.

JANE SEYMOUR

There is only one thing more painful
than learning from experience
and that is not learning from experience.

ARCHIBALD MCLEISH

SEPTEMBER **17**

One must learn to care for oneself first,
so that one can then dare
to care for someone else.

MAYA ANGELOU

APRIL 17

Happiness,
not in another place
but this place...
not for another hour,
but this hour.

WALT WHITMAN

Anyone can carry their burden,
however hard, until nightfall.
Anyone can do their work,
however hard, for one day.
Anyone can live sweetly, patiently,
lovingly, purely,
till the sun goes down.

ROBERT LOUIS STEVENSON

Never, if possible, lie down at night
without being able to say:
"I have made one human being
at least a little wiser, or a little happier,
or a little better this day."

CHARLES KINGSLEY

SEPTEMBER **19**

The most wasted day of all is that
on which we have not laughed.

SEBASTIEN NICOLAS CHAMFORT

APRIL **15**

No more brooding,
No more despondency.
Your life will become
The beauty of a rose,
The song of the dawn,
The dance of twilight.

SRI CHINMOY

THE GREATEST
OF ALL CAPABILITIES
OF A HUMAN BEING
IS TO BECOME
BORN AGAIN.

J. R. RIM

We shall draw
from the heart of suffering the means
of inspiration and survival.

SIR WINSTON CHURCHILL

SEPTEMBER **21**

Only as high as I reach can I grow,
Only as far as I seek can I go,
Only as deep as I look can I see,
Only as much as I dream can I be.

KAREN RAVN

Don't be afraid of failure.
Be more afraid of not trying... take chances and risks –
not foolhardy actions but actions
which could result in failure,
yet promise success and great reward.

COLIN L. POWELL

SEPTEMBER **22**

Caretake this moment. Immerse yourself in its particulars.
Respond to this person, this challenge, this deed.
Quit the evasions. Stop giving yourself needless trouble.
It is time to really live; to fully inhabit
the situation you happen to be in now.

EPICTETUS   APRIL **12**

THE COURAGE
OF ENDURANCE
FAR OUTWEIGHS
SUDDEN BRAVERY.

ODILE DORMEUIL

In today's world
full of agony and pain,
we have no choice
but to equip ourselves
with the patience
and hope that will see us to
the safest shore.

ZIYAD ALAWNEH

Don't be afraid of new beginnings.
Don't shy away from new people,
new energy, new surroundings.
Embrace new chances at happiness.

AUTHOR UNKNOWN

SEPTEMBER **24**

WHAT DOES NOT DESTROY ME, MAKES ME STRONG.

FRIEDRICH WILHELM NIETZSCHE

We get one go this side of eternity, one go!
It's not a dress rehearsal, it's one go and you make
the most of it and you take opportunities
that come along that you like and you go for it.

ANN WIDDECOMBE

SEPTEMBER 25

The best things are nearest: breath in your nostrils, light in your eyes, flowers at your feet, duties at your hand, the path of Right just before you. Do not grasp at the stars, but do life's plain common work as it comes, certain that daily duties and daily bread are the sweetest things in life.

ROBERT LOUIS STEVENSON

You can defeat fear through humour, through pain, through honesty, bravery, intuition, and through love in the truest sense.

JOHN CASSAVETES

SEPTEMBER **26**

One day you will
wake up and there won't
be any more time
to do the things
you've always wanted.
Do it now.

PAULO COELHO

The secret of making something work
in your life is, first of all, the deep desire to make it work:
then the faith and belief that it can work:
then to hold that clear definite vision in your consciousness
and see it working out step by step,
without one thought of doubt or disbelief.

EILEEN CADDY

SEPTEMBER 27

Yesterday
is a cancelled cheque;
tomorrow
is a promissory note;
today
is the only cash you have –
so spend it wisely.

KAY LYONS

Fear keeps you awake and aware.
It's an ally. Treat it with respect.
Courage is not absence of fear – courage is
recognising fear and operating in spite of it.
Fear is an ally that empowers us.

STUART WILDE

SEPTEMBER **28**

What we vividly imagine,
ardently desire, enthusiastically act upon,
must inevitably come to pass.

COLIN P. SISSON

Hope doesn't die in winter,
hope grows in winter.
It's the most difficult
circumstances of life,
the winter seasons of life,
that give rise to
the strongest hope.

WOODROW KROLL

The secret of our being
is not only to live but to
have something to live for,
something towards
which to strive,
something to become.

PAUL S. MCELROY

You can have the courage to climb the mountain,
swim the lakes, go on a raft to the other side
of the Atlantic or Pacific. That, any fool can do,
but the courage to be on your own,
to stand on your two solid feet, is something which
cannot be given by somebody.

U. G. KRISHNAMURTI

Events will take their
course, it is no good
of being angry at them;
they are happiest
who wisely turns them
to the best account.

EURIPIDES

To hope is to risk disappointment.
But risks must be taken because the greatest
risk in life is to risk nothing.

WILLIAM ARTHUR WARD

OCTOBER 1

You can, you know,
just choose to be happy.
Why not? Keep telling yourself
you are and you will be.
It's not really that hard to do.
And, here's the thing,
if you choose to be happy
it makes others happier and so
it goes around and around.
On and on.

DALTON EXLEY

THE BEGINNING IS ALWAYS TODAY.

MARY WOLLSTONECRAFT SHELLEY

A positive attitude causes
a chain reaction of
positive thoughts, events
and outcomes.
It is a catalyst and it sparks
extraordinary results.

WADE BOGGS

I have always believed that,
no matter how dark the cloud, there is always a thin,
silver lining, and that is what we must look for.
The silver lining will come...

WANGARI MAATHAI

OCTOBER **3**

Twenty years from now you will be more disappointed
by the things that you didn't do than the ones you did do.
So throw off the bowlines. Sail away from safe harbor.
Catch the trade winds in your sails. Explore. Dream. Discover.

MARK TWAIN

APRIL 1

In the hour of adversity
be not without hope,
for crystal rain falls from
black clouds.

PERSIAN PROVERB

The great danger
for most of us is not
that our aim is too high
and we miss,
but that it is too low
and we achieve it.

MICHELANGELO

To awaken each morning with a smile brightening my face;
to greet the day with reverence for the opportunities
it contains; to approach my work with a clean mind;
to hold ever before me, even in the doing of little things, the
ultimate purpose toward which I am working; to meet
men and women with laughter on my lips and love
in my heart; to be gentle, kind, and courteous through
all the hours; to approach the night with weariness that
ever woos sleep and the joy that comes from work well done
– this is how I desire to waste wisely my days.

THOMAS DEKKER

Love bravely, live bravely,
be courageous.
There's really
nothing to lose.
There's no wrong you
can't make right again.

JEWEL KILCHER

It's a funny thing about life,
once you begin to take
note of the things
you are grateful for,
you begin to lose sight of the
things that you lack.

GERMANY KENT

Our people get tromped on, stepped on, and lied to –
the whole works – but you can't dwell on pain.
That is the past. With all of us working for a better
tomorrow, things can get better. If we dwell on all hurts,
nothing will come of it except hard feelings.
We have enough of those. We have to work for a better
tomorrow and for all the pain to heal in our spirits.

MILDRED KALAMA IKEBE

Gratitude unlocks the fullness of life. It turns
what we have into enough, and more.
It turns denial into acceptance, chaos into order,
confusion to clarity. It can turn a meal into a feast,
a house into a home, a stranger into a friend.
Gratitude makes sense of our past, brings
peace for today, and creates vision for tomorrow.

MELODY BEATTIE

People create their own
questions because they're
afraid to look straight.
All you have to do is
look straight and see the road,
and when you see it,
don't sit looking at it – walk.

AYN RAND

Y ou will get all you want in life
if you help enough
other people get what they want.

ZIG ZIGLAR

OCTOBER 8

...misfortune and
destruction are not final.
When the grass
has been burnt by the fire
of the steppe, it will grow
anew in summer.

MONGOLIAN WISDOM

We should be
as water, which
is lower
than all things
yet stronger
even than the rocks.

OGLALA SIOUX

Try to hold on.
Everyone holds a secret
store of courage,
Hidden away till times
like these. Come.
Time to turn the key.

PAM BROWN

Surround yourself with only people
who are going to lift you higher.

OPRAH WINFREY

OCTOBER **10**

Oh, my friend,
it's not what they
take away from you
that counts.
It's what you do
with what you have left.

HUBERT H. HUMPHREY

Trust yourself. Create the kind
of self that you will be happy
to live with all your life.
Make the most of yourself
by fanning the tiny,
inner sparks of possibility
into flames of achievement.

GOLDA MEIR

If you want to be happy, be.
Stop a moment, cease your work, look around you.

LEO TOLSTOY

Change can be scary, but you know what's scarier?
Allowing fear to stop you from growing, evolving and progressing.

MANDY HALE

OCTOBER **12**

We all get report cards in many different ways, but
the real excitement of what you're doing is in the doing of it.
It's not what you're going to get in the end.
It's not the final curtain.
It's really in the doing it and loving what you're doing.

RALPH LAUREN

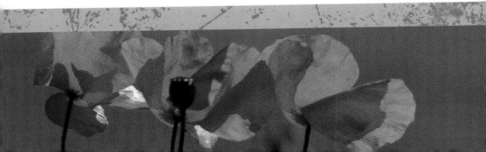

It's during those dark times,
those knock-down-drag-out hard incidents,
when it seems there's no way out,
no light at the end of the tunnel,
that one mere thought can not only take root,
not only blossom, but pull you through
and actually propel you to the other side.
And all you have to do is believe.

DAVE PELZER

Through our thoughts
we are gaining power or losing it.
Positive thoughts generate power,
negative ones waste it.

DADI JANKI

We should be blessed if we lived in the present always,
and took advantage of every accident that befell us,
like the grass which confesses the influence
of the slightest dew that falls on it; and did not spend
our time in atoning for the neglect of past opportunities...
we loiter in winter while it is already spring.

HENRY DAVID THOREAU

OCTOBER **14**

The thing I love
about the human spirit
is that no matter
how dire the circumstances –
there always comes a point
when you can have a laugh and
forget about what is
happening for a minute –
realise you're still alive
and all things are possible.

CARON KEATING

What a new face courage
puts on everything!
...courage comes to my rescue,
gives strength to my body,
conquers danger, and makes
all things possible.

AUTHOR UNKNOWN

Life engenders life.
Energy creates energy.
It is by spending oneself
that one becomes rich.

SARAH BERNHARDT

Every time you are tempted to react in
the same old way, ask if you want to be a prisoner
of the past or a pioneer of the future.

DEEPAK CHOPRA

OCTOBER **16**

MARCH **19**

The way may be blocked.
Do not despair, look about you.
There are side roads that you never noticed.
Tracks hidden in the undergrowth.
Try. Explore. And find the path
to lead you on at last.

PAM BROWN

To greet a lovely morning, we must leave the night behind.

TARANG SINHA

OCTOBER **17**

MARCH **18**

There is no passion
to be found
playing small – in settling
for a life that's less
than the one
you're capable of living.

NELSON ROLIHLAHLA MANDELA

NOTHING
IS WORTH
MORE
THAN THIS DAY.

JOHANN WOLFGANG VON GOETHE

With courage you will
dare to take risks,
have the strength to be
compassionate and
the wisdom to be humble.
Courage is the
foundation of integrity.

KESHAVAN NAIR

In a battle, or in mountain climbing, there is often one thing which it takes a lot of pluck to do; but it is also, in the long run, the safest thing to do. If you funk it, you will find yourself, hours later, in far worse danger. The cowardly thing is also the most dangerous thing.

C. S. LEWIS

OCTOBER **19**

YOU MUST NEVER BE FEARFUL ABOUT WHAT YOU ARE DOING WHEN IT IS RIGHT.

ROSA PARKS

YOUR LIFE
DOES NOT GET
BETTER
BY CHANCE.
IT GETS BETTER
BY CHANGE.

JIM ROHN

The Ancient Greeks told us that someone that finds discontentment in one place is not likely to find happiness in another. It's as old as time. Happiness isn't something we can get from owning something. Or moving somewhere. Happiness is how we see life. How it fills us. Is beyond us. How it passes through our children, into new lives. Into everything. This is happiness.

DALTON EXLEY

Every day has a new possibility.
Every day you can improve yourself and grow.
Every day you can take yourself to a new level. Grab something
with momentum that you can be passionate about.
Keep working on it and amazing things will happen.

BILL ZANKER

Whenever someone has found the courage
to live more deeply, more courageously than before,
no matter how short a time it may be,
they hold open that door for anyone who tries to follow.

RACHEL NAOMI REMEN

Every dream we have
represents a seed.
You have to take
that seed and plant it,
nurture it,
wait for it to grow.

MICA PARIS

THE STRONGER YOUR VALUES AND COMMITMENT, THE EASIER THE ROAD.

MONICA PRABAR PILAR

Physical bravery is an animal instinct;
moral bravery is much higher and truer courage.

WENDELL PHILLIPS

OCTOBER 23

The simple things
Are often best:
A simple,
Helping hand,
A kindly thought,
The simple phrase,
"Of course, I understand."

ANNE KREER

If you believe you can do
something, you can.
There is only one way.
With very good attitude,
positive thinking,
hard work and dedication.
With these four
things together.

SEVERIANO BALLESTEROS

If you want to achieve something,
vaguely hoping that somehow it'll turn out
means that it probably won't.
If you want something so badly it's worth fighting for,
then add focus, dedication and hard work
to your hope and you'll be in with a chance.

DALTON EXLEY

No, this is not the beginning
of a new chapter in my life;
this is the beginning of a new book!
That first book is already closed, ended,
and tossed into the seas; this new
book is newly opened, has just begun!
Look, it is the first page!
And it is a beautiful one!

C. JOYBELL C.

Throughout
the centuries
there were people
who took first steps,
down new roads,
armed with nothing
but their own vision.

AYN RAND

The road to our goal may be long.
Sometimes you may feel that you are on an endless road
through a barren desert, and that the goal
is still impossibly far away. But do not give up walking
just because the distance seems far.
You have to be a divine soldier
and march on bravely and untiringly.

SRI CHINMOY

OCTOBER **26**

Every day, think as you wake up:
Today I am fortunate to have woken up.
I am alive. I have a precious human life.
I am not going to waste it.

THE DALAI LAMA

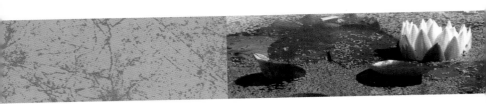

When you feel that you have reached the end and that you cannot go one step further, when life seems to be drained of all purpose: What a wonderful opportunity to start all over again, to turn over a new page.

EILEEN CADDY

My will has been tested, my courage has been tested, my strength has been tested. Now my patience and endurance are being tested... I have learned to live my life one step, one breath, and one moment at a time, but it was a long road. I set out on a journey of love, seeking truth, peace, and understanding. I am still learning.

MUHAMMAD ALI

Everyone has been
made for some particular
work, and the desire
for that work has been
put in every heart.

JALAL AL-DIN MUHAMMAD RUMI

We MUST ACCEPT
FINITE DISAPPOINTMENT,
BUT WE MUST
NEVER LOSE
INFINITE HOPE.

MARTIN LUTHER KING JR.

The opposite of love
is not hate, it's indifference.
The opposite of art
is not ugliness, it's indifference.
The opposite of faith
is not heresy, it's indifference.
And the opposite of life
is not death, it's indifference.

ELIE WIESEL

What is the best gift
you ever received?
Better still, what is the best
gift you ever gave?
Perhaps you will recall that
in each instance,
the best gift was one...
that included a part of self.

WANDA FULTON

At the end
of anyone's tunnel,
the glaring light
is a wonderful thing.

DAME KELLY HOLMES

We have a saying: "The lotus grows in the mud."…
The lotus is the most beautiful flower, whose petals open
one by one. But it will only grow in mud. In order to grow
and gain wisdom, first you must have the mud –
the obstacles of life and its suffering…
The mud speaks of the common ground that we humans
share, no matter what our stations in life…

KUTENLA, BUDDHIST MONK

MARCH **5**

Just because you fall off a horse, you don't have to lie there. If all you can do is crawl, then crawl. If you can get up, walk. If you have to limp, find something to lean on and keep going. Never say, "This is it," and give up.

BEAR HEART (MUSKOGEE)

The greater part
of this world's
bravery is hidden.
No accolades.
No medals.
Silent endurance,
unrecognised.

PAM BROWN

Our own worst enemy
cannot harm us
as much as our
unwise thoughts.
No one can help us
as much as our own
compassionate thoughts.

GAUTAMA BUDDHA

Never give up, because
you never know
what the tide will bring in the next day.

TOM HANKS

Quieten your mind
and close your eyes.
Be still. Feel the sun
upon your face.
Hear the shrill of bird song.
Rejoice in your senses.
Rejoice in life.

PAM BROWN

Hope can make the present moment
less difficult to bear.
If we believe that tomorrow will be better,
we can bear a hardship today.

THICH NHAT HANH

MARCH 2

Wisdom comes most easily to those who
have the courage to embrace life without judgement
and are willing to not know... Wisdom requires us
to be more fully and simply alive than we have been taught to be.
It may require us to suffer. But ultimately
we will be more than we were when we began.

RACHEL NAOMI REMEN

NOVEMBER **3**

I am emerging from an ocean of grief,
From the sorrow of many deaths,
From the inevitability of tragedy,
I am seeing the living that is to be lived,
The laughter that is to be laughed,
The loving that is to be accomplished.
I am learning at last
that tremendous triumph of life.

MARJORIE PIZER

The walls we erect around ourselves,
with bricks made of fear,
are well-nigh impenetrable.
Cowering behind them, we become
prejudiced, ignorant and inert...
It takes a supreme effort to breach
those barricades of your conditioning...
To move through the various stages of
life takes courage. And determination.

SHEILA HANCOCK

Remember, all
the answers you need
are inside of you;
you only have to
become quiet enough
to hear them.

DEBBIE FORD

IF YOU ARE
GOING THROUGH HELL,
KEEP GOING.

AUTHOR UNKNOWN

To have lived long enough to see the sun, the dapple of leaves, star-studded skies and kindly faces – to have heard the wind, bird song, loving voices, to have touched a little cat, a woollen blanket, a flower, to have tasted clear water, fresh bread, honey, to have breathed the perfume of a rose is enough to make any life worth the living.

CHARLOTTE GRAY

FEBRUARY **27**

Isn't it nice to think
that tomorrow
is a new day
with no mistakes in it yet?

LUCY MAUD MONTGOMERY

BE WILLING
TO BE
A BEGINNER
EVERY SINGLE
MORNING.

MEISTER ECKHART

Wake up
with a smile and
go after life…
live it, enjoy it, taste it,
smell it, feel it.

JOE KNAPP

I wanted you to see what
real courage is, instead of getting
the idea that courage is a man
with a gun in his hand.
It's when you know you're licked
before you begin but you begin
anyway and you see it through
no matter what.

HARPER LEE

The thought that we are enduring
the unendurable
is one of the things that keep us going.

MOLLY HASKELL

NOVEMBER **8**

Though no one
can go back and make
a brand new start,
anyone can start now
and make
a brand new ending.

CARL BARD

Set goals
that make you feel
powerful, motivated,
and driven when you
focus on them.

STEVE PAVLINA

Stay positive and happy.
Work hard and don't
give up hope.
Be open to criticism
and keep learning.
Surround yourself
with happy, warm
and genuine people.

TENA DESAE

Perhaps the most important thing we bring
to another person is the silence in us. Not the sort of silence
that is filled with unspoken criticism or hard withdrawal.
The sort of silence that is a place of refuge, or rest,
of acceptance of someone as they are.

RACHEL NAOMI REMEN

NOVEMBER **10**

CARVE A TUNNEL OF HOPE THROUGH THE DARK MOUNTAIN OF DISAPPOINTMENT.

MARTIN LUTHER KING JR.

FEBRUARY **22**

THE
UNENDURABLE
IS THE
BEGINNING
OF THE CURVE
OF JOY.

DJUNA BARNES

Work hard for what you want because it won't come to you without a fight. You have to be strong and courageous and know that you can do anything you put your mind to. If somebody puts you down or criticizes you, just keep on believing in yourself and turn it into something positive.

LEAH LABELLE

FEBRUARY **21**

Determine
to live life with flair
and laughter.

MAYA ANGELOU

NOVEMBER **12**

We cannot escape fear.
We only transform it
into a companion that accompanies
us on all our exciting adventures…
Take a risk a day –
one small or bold stroke
that will make you feel great
once you have done it.

SUSAN JEFFERS

I will not let
anyone
walk through
my mind
with their dirty feet.

MAHATMA GANDHI

The longer I live, the more I realise the impact of attitude on my life. Attitude to me, is more important than facts. It is more important than the past, than education, than money, than circumstances, than failures, than successes, than what other people think or say or do. It is more important than appearances, giftedness or skill. It will make or break a company... a church... a home.

CHARLES SWINDOLL

FEBRUARY **19**

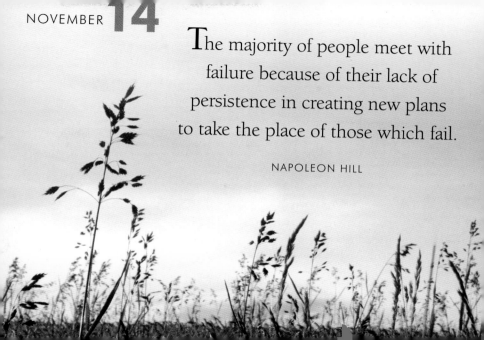

The majority of people meet with failure because of their lack of persistence in creating new plans to take the place of those which fail.

NAPOLEON HILL

What you possess, what you earn, what you're worth,
these things over time mean less and less, till like
a grain of sand on a beach that's hardly discernible.
What you give, who you love, how you're loved and what you
really love, these are the things that really matter in the end.
Don't wait till you're about done to realise this.
Recognise it now, live it now.
And be a little thankful you didn't leave it any later.

DALTON EXLEY

Never look down
to test the ground
before taking your next step:
only they who keep
their eyes fixed
on the far horizon
will find the right road.

DAG HAMMARSKJÖLD

It does not matter
how long you are spending
on the earth, how much
money you have gathered
or how much attention
you have received.
It is the amount
of positive vibration
you have radiated in life
that matters.

AMIT RAY

ALL HUMAN
WISDOM
IS SUMMED UP
IN TWO WORDS –
WAIT AND HOPE.

ALEXANDRE DUMAS

Become a possibilitarian.
No matter how dark things seem to be
or actually are, raise your sights
and see the possibilities –
always see them, for they're always there.

NORMAN VINCENT PEALE

FEBRUARY **16**

Courage is a spark
that can become
the flame of hope,
lighting new
and exciting pathways
in what seemed to be dead,
dark landscapes.

JOHN O'DONOHUE

You must learn day by day,
year by year,
to broaden your horizon.
The more things you love,
the more you are interested in,
the more you enjoy,
the more you are indignant about –
the more you have left
when anything happens.

ETHEL BARRYMORE

When you realise
there is nothing lacking,
the whole world belongs to you.

LAO TZU   NOVEMBER **18**

When you are worn, when you are battered, when you feel worse for wear, find a way to look beyond these temporary illusions to the grand vision of your life.

These feelings are what feed you; they are the motivation underlying your future greatness, exposed for you to examine.

JAIME MORRISON CURTIS

FEBRUARY **14**

Each time someone stands up for
an ideal or acts to improve the lot of others
or strikes out against injustice, he sends
forth a tiny ripple of hope, and crossing
each other from a million different centers
of energy and daring, those ripples build a
current that can sweep down the mightiest
walls of oppression and resistance.

ROBERT F. KENNEDY JR.

You have powers you never
dreamed of. You can do things
you never thought you could do.
There are no limitations
in what you can do except
the limitations in your own mind
as to what you cannot do.
Don't think you cannot.
Think you can.

DARWIN P. KINGSLEY

Life is not what we think –
it's not even what we make it. There's so much else
and ultimately we can only love each other –
help each other and extend that as much as we can.
THAT'S IT. See that we are all one, no matter
what is happening. Have compassion –
what else have we got? Faith, love, trust, just love.

CARON KEATING

In Chinese,
the symbol for
the word "crisis"
has two meanings:
danger and
opportunity.

DOUGLAS KENNEDY

You will never realise your best
destiny through the avoidance of fear.
Rather, you will realise it through
the exercise of courage,
which means taking whatever action
is most liberating to the soul,
even when you are afraid.

MARTHA BECK

It's humbling to start fresh.
It takes a lot of courage.
But it can be reinvigorating.
You just have to put
your ego on a shelf
and tell it to be quiet.

JENNIFER RITCHIE PAYETTE

For people sometimes believed that it was safer
to live with complaints, was necessary
to cooperate with grief, was all right to become
an accomplice in self-ambush... Take heart to flat out decide
to be well and stride into the future sane and whole.

TONI CADE BAMBARA

To STILL HOLD ON WHEN HOPE IS GONE
IS THE GREATEST FORM OF COURAGE.

PAM BROWN

The magic in new beginnings
is truly the most powerful of them all.

JOSIYAH MARTIN

Live with intention. Walk to the edge.
Listen hard. Practice wellness.
Play with abandon. Laugh. Choose with no regret.
Do what you love. Live as if this is all there is.

MARY ANNE RADMACHER

SUCCESS
IS FALLING
NINE TIMES
AND GETTING UP.

JON BON JOVI

The shock of failure, of disappointments, of betrayal, hits like a physical blow. Breathless and blinded, you lose all contact with the life you lived till now – the ordinary life that seemed untouchable. Hold fast. However impossible it seems that happiness and certainty will return – they will, they will. A thousand voices tell you so – speaking from hard experience.

ODILE DORMEUIL

If I had my life to live over... I'd dare
to make more mistakes next time.
I'd relax. I would limber up. I would be sillier than
I have been this trip. I would take fewer things seriously.
I would take more chances. I would climb
more mountains and swim more rivers.
I would perhaps have more actual troubles,
But I'd have fewer imaginary ones.

NADINE STAIR

What is the difference
between an obstacle
and an opportunity?
Our attitude toward it.
Every opportunity has
a difficulty, and every
difficulty has an opportunity.

J. SIDLOW BAXTER

Those who face
irrevocable suffering with
a quiet mind and are able
to take pleasures in the little
joys still left to them –
they are the truly brave.

PAM BROWN

We perceive that only through
utter defeat are we able to take our
first steps towards liberation and strength.
Our admissions of personal
powerlessness finally turn out to be
a firm bedrock upon which
happy and purposeful lives may be built.

BILL WILSON

LET THE BEAUTY
WE LOVE
BE WHAT WE DO.

JALAL AL-DIN MUHAMMAD RUMI

It is a terrible thing, this kindness that human beings do not lose.
Terrible because when we are finally naked in the dark and cold,
it is all we have. We who are so rich, so full of strength,
wind up with that small change. We have nothing else to give.

URSULA K. LE GUIN

Hardships and handicaps can... stimulate our energy to survive them. You'll find if you study the lives of other people who've accomplished things, it's often been done with the help of great willpower in overcoming things.

BEATRICE WOOD

It's often possible to turn negative situations into positive.
Never feel a situation is all negative.
There's a counterpart that is positive.
Look for it, reach for it, utilize it – it will offset the negative.

BEAR HEART (MUSKOGEE)

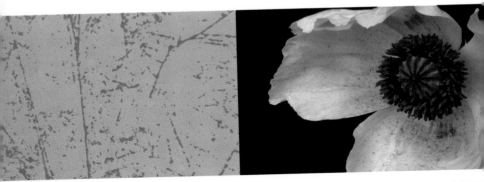

Things are going wrong.
You feel low, a failure…
SMILE! Bare your teeth
if you can't smile from inside.
Fake it if you have to.
Everyone you see
will feel better –
and so will you.

JODIE "BUBBLES" ALAN

The most complete
happiness is to work
at something you love,
and to do it to the best
of your ability.

ODILE DORMEUIL

Is there any symbol more redolent of regeneration
than a seed, planted in rich compost, watered and warmed,
to produce a new shoot of green in the spring,
crowned by two perky, embryonic leaves? A tiny start,
with the promise of plenty. It has taken me a long time
to learn to look at those little leaves, and appreciate
their significance, but I understand it now.
And it has saved me from depression, even despair.

BARNEY BARDSLEY

Challenges
are what make life
interesting;
overcoming them
is what makes life
meaningful.

JOSHUA J. MARINE

Many of my AIDS patients discovered
that the last year of their lives was
by far their best. Many have said they
wouldn't have traded the rich quality
of that last year of life
for a healthier body. Sadly, it is only
when tragedy strikes
that most of us begin attending to
the deeper aspects of life.

ELISABETH KÜBLER-ROSS

If I were asked to give
what I consider the single most useful
bit of advice for all humanity
it would be this:
Expect trouble as an inevitable part of life
and when it comes, hold your head high,
look it squarely in the eye and say,
"I will be bigger than you.
You cannot defeat me."

ANN LANDERS

All of us experience fear, but when we confront and acknowledge it, we are able to turn it into courage. Being courageous does not mean never being scared; it means acting as you know you must even though you are undeniably afraid.

ARCHBISHOP DESMOND TUTU

DECEMBER **2**

Be thankful
for what you have,
you'll end up
having more.
If you concentrate on
what you don't have,
you will never,
ever have enough.

OPRAH WINFREY

The fact that courage
is expected of you
in the face of the unbearable
gives you strength for
the rest of your life.

NELSON ROLIHLAHLA MANDELA

To CONQUER
ANYTHING
ONE FEARED
IS LIBERATION,
EXALTATION.
UTTER JOY.

PAMELA DUGDALE

FORGET INJURIES,
NEVER FORGET KINDNESS.

CONFUCIUS

Happiness does not come
from doing easy work,
but from the afterglow
of satisfaction that comes
after the achievement
of a difficult task
that demanded our best.

THEODORE I. RUBIN

WHEN DARKNESS
IS AT ITS DARKEST,
THAT IS THE BEGINNING
OF ALL LIGHT.

LAO TSE

Courage. That's a big word. Powerful. Intense. Intimidating. It's a word for heroes, for those who brave the impossible, who live bigger than life.

KATHERINE MARTIN

Stop for a moment during the day and let the sun bathe your face. Take a second or two to listen to the music of the laughter of your children as they play.

Go to a river bank and listen to the sound of the water, the chirping birds, the blowing of the wind. It is the world around you that speaks to you, that will inspire you.

If you listen hard enough, you will find the voice within yourself, and the ability and the power to make a difference.

ERIN BROCKOVICH

We each hold within us
a scrap of stardust.
Whatever dark engulfs us,
nothing can put out its light.
Whatever foolishness
distracts us, it alone is constant.
It seeks the shining that exists
in everything that lives.

PAM BROWN

WE MAY ENCOUNTER
MANY DEFEATS,
BUT WE MUST NOT
BE DEFEATED.

MAYA ANGELOU

Under the sound and fury of a pandemic
is the enduring courage of people.
Silent but strong.
Holding to life in hope of better days.

MAYA V. PATEL

JANUARY **26**

Write the bad things
that are done to you in sand, but
write the good things that happen to you
on a piece of marble.

ARAB PROVERB

Usually the most amazing
things come along after
the hardest times,
so hold on in the storm
and trust that
when it finally passes you'll
have your time in the sun.

MICA PARIS

The true test of a character
is to face hard conditions
with the determination
to make them better.

HELEN KELLER
(BORN BOTH DEAF AND BLIND)

Begin doing what you want to do now. We are not living
in eternity. We have only this moment, sparkling
like a star in our hand – and melting like a snowflake.

SIR FRANCIS BACON

One of the best safeguards of our hopes...
is to be able to mark off the areas of
hopelessness and to acknowledge them,
to face them directly, not with despair but with
the creative intent of keeping them from
polluting all the areas of possibility.

WILLIAM F. LYNCH

LIFE IS A TRAGEDY FULL OF JOY.

BERNARD MALAMUD

NOTHING IN LIFE IS TO BE FEARED. IT IS ONLY TO BE UNDERSTOOD.

MARIE CURIE

Often, we tend to impose our own greatest limitations. We are the ones who limit what we think we're capable of doing. But sometimes, if you blow that top off and really dream, you can accomplish, build, and grow a life far beyond anything you had ever imagined.

JARED KUSHNER

Not everything
that is faced
can be changed,
but nothing
can be changed
until it is faced.

JAMES BALDWIN

Out of every crisis comes
the chance to be reborn,
to reconceive ourselves
as individuals,
to choose the kind
of change that will help
us to grow and to fulfil
ourselves more completely.

NENA O'NEILL

Repeat to yourself
the most comforting
of all words,
"This too shall pass."

ANN LANDERS

Often people attempt to live their lives backwards:
they try to have more things, or more money,
in order to do more of what they want so they will be happier.
The way it actually works is the reverse. You must first be
who you really are, then do what you need to do,
in order to have what you want.

MARGARET YOUNG   JANUARY **20**

There is no dress rehearsal for life.
This is it. This is life.
Play it to the fullest!

SCOUT CLOUD LEE, NATIVE AMERICAN

DECEMBER 14

Sometimes, when the sun goes down,
It seems it will never rise again...
But it will!

Sometimes, when you feel alone,
It seems your heart will break in two...
But it won't.

And sometimes it seems
It's hardly worth carrying on...
But it is.

FRANK BROWN

Adversity assails us
with hurricane force.
Glowing sunrises are
transformed into darkest nights.
Our hugest hopes are
blasted and our noblest
dreams are shattered.

MARTIN LUTHER KING JR.

Press on. Nothing can take the place of perseverance. Talent will not. Nothing is more common than unsuccessful men and women with talent. Genius will not. Unrewarded genius is almost a proverb. Education will not. The world is full of educated derelicts. Persistence and determination alone are omnipotent. This slogan "press on" has solved, always will solve, the problems of the human race.

CALVIN COOLIDGE

When you push a bulb deep into soft wet soil,
it is always a symbol of hope – hope that nature
will not fail; hope that you will still be alive to see the bulb
burst out of the ground and unfurl its delicate leaves,
opening the way for the flower. It is about a future you can
only hope for: maybe you won't see the flower
in all its glory, but someone will.

ROSIE BOYCOTT

DECEMBER **16**

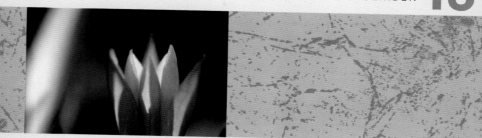

Starting over is an acceptance
of a past we can't change,
an unrelenting conviction
that the future can be different,
and the stubborn wisdom to use
the past to make the future
what the past was not.

CRAIG D. LOUNSBROUGH

The bravest thing
you can do when you
are not brave is to
profess courage
and act accordingly.

CORRA MAY WHITE HARRIS

I learned that courage was not the absence of fear,
but the triumph over it.
The brave person is not the one who does not feel afraid,
but the one who conquers that fear.

NELSON ROLIHLAHLA MANDELA

DECEMBER **18**

Courage and perseverance have
a magical talisman, before which difficulties
disappear, and obstacles vanish into air.

JOHN QUINCY ADAMS

We ought to remember that we are not the only
ones to find ourselves at an apparent impasse.
Just as a kite rises against the wind,
even the worst of troubles can strengthen us.
As thousands before us have met the identical fate
and mastered it, so can we!

DR. R. BRASCH

JANUARY **15**

We must live through the dreary winter
if we would value the spring.
And the woods must be cold
and silent before the robins sing.
The flowers must be buried in darkness
before they can bud and bloom.
And the sweetest, warmest sunshine comes
after the storm and gloom.

AUTHOR UNKNOWN

In the darkest moments of your own life,
never lose sight of the fact that the sun
is going to shine through to a great day, a great life.
Whatever your potential is, you can reach it.

BEAR HEART (MUSKOGEE)

Walk on a rainbow trail; walk on a trail of song.
And all about you will be beauty.
There is a way out of every dark mist,
over a rainbow trail.

NAVAJO SONG

We learn the most through our mistakes, not our successes. And we grow the most in tough times. If you can get your head around this and see tough times as a chance for growth and deeper meaning, you will arm yourself with the most powerful mental weapon known to man – optimism.

GARY PLAYER

JANUARY **13**

You gotta stick it out, because there's only one
ball-game here, and it's your own life. You got no choice.
You got to play to win if you want to stay on this earth.

CANCER PATIENT

DECEMBER **21**

Enthusiasm is
everything.
It must be taut
and vibrating like
a guitar string.

PELÉ

HOPE IS
A POWERFUL
WEAPON
EVEN WHEN
NOTHING ELSE
MAY REMAIN.

NELSON ROLIHLAHLA MANDELA

If life teaches us anything,
it's maybe that it's necessary
to suffer some defeats.
Look at a diamond:
it is the result of extreme pressure.
Less pressure, it is a crystal;
less than that, it's coal;
and less than that, it is fossilized
leaves or just plain dirt.

MAYA ANGELOU

If the future seems overwhelming,
remember that it comes
one moment at a time.

BETH MENDE CONNY

Work like
you don't need
the money,
love like your heart
has never been broken
and dance like
no one is
watching.

LARRY MCMURTRY

TURN YOUR WOUNDS INTO WISDOM.

OPRAH WINFREY

JANUARY **9**

Every day is a fresh beginning.
Every morn is the world made new.

SARAH CHAUNCEY WOOLSEY

I have found that
there is a tremendous joy in giving.
It is a very important part
of the joy of living.

WILLIAM BLACK

DECEMBER **25**

JANUARY **8**

Believe you can and you're halfway there.

THEODORE ROOSEVELT

It seems to me that we can
never give up longing and wishing
while we are thoroughly alive.
There are certain things we feel
to be beautiful and good,
and we must hunger after them.

GEORGE ELIOT (MARY ANN EVANS)

Life is a bowl of cherries. Some cherries are rotten while others are good; it's your job to throw out the rotten ones and forget about them while you enjoy eating the ones that are good!

There are two kinds of people: those who choose to throw out the good cherries and wallow in all the rotten ones, and those who choose to throw out all the rotten ones and savor all the good ones.

C. JOYBELL C.

JANUARY **7**

Pursue some path, however
narrow and crooked, in which
you can walk with love and reverence.

HENRY DAVID THOREAU

"There is no hope"
is a sickening blow –
and yet we still go on.
The human heart survives
in its resilience.

PAM BROWN

When I'm old and dying, I plan to look back on my life and say "Wow, that was an adventure" not "Wow, I sure felt safe."

TOM PRESTON-WERNER

Courage is amazing because it can tap into
the heart of fear, taking that frightened energy
and turning it towards initiative, creativity,
action and hope. When courage comes alive,
imprisoning walls become frontiers of new possibilities,
difficulty becomes invitation and the heart
comes into a new rhythm of trust and sureness.

JOHN O'DONOHUE

…there is no obstacle
you cannot surmount,
no challenge you cannot meet,
no fear you cannot conquer,
no matter how impossible
it may sometimes seem.

ERIN BROCKOVICH

JANUARY **4**

Although time seems
to fly by,
it never travels faster
than one day at a time.
Each day
is a new opportunity
to live your life
to the fullest.

STEVE MARABOLI

No matter what happens,
or how bad it seems today,
life does go on,
and it will be better tomorrow.

MAYA ANGELOU

No matter what happens,
no matter what challenges life brings,
you have to just take a few big breaths,
believe in yourself,
and pick yourself back up.
If things are bad and
it's hard to be alive…
well, things will get better.
You really just have to believe it.
That's all. You have to believe.

OKSANA BAIUL

Enjoy the little things of life.
There may come a time
when you realise
they were the big things.

ROBERT BRAULT

DECEMBER 31

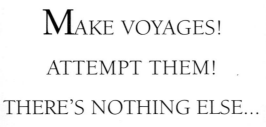

Make voyages!

ATTEMPT THEM!

THERE'S NOTHING ELSE...

TENNESSEE WILLIAMS

If you love this book…
you will probably want to know how to find
other Helen Exley® books like it. They're all listed on

www.helenexley.com

The Helen Exley® LONDON Daily quotations books
cover the most powerful relationships: the love between couples,
and the bonds within families or between friends.
A very strong theme in Helen's books is wisdom, calm and personal values.
Her team of researchers spare no expense in making sure
each book is as thoughtful and meaningful as it is possible to create;
good to give and good to receive. You have the results in your hands.
If you find the quotes in INSPIRATION helpful, please tell others.
There is no power like a word-of-mouth recommendation (or a tweet!).

You can follow us on and

IMPORTANT COPYRIGHT NOTICE
The publishers are grateful for permission to reproduce copyright material. Whilst every effort has been made
to trace copyright holders, we would be pleased to hear from any not here acknowledged.

Get interested in something. Get enthralled.
The more you lose yourself in something
bigger than yourself, the more energy you will have.

NORMAN VINCENT PEALE

PHOTOGRAPHY BY RICHARD EXLEY
EDITED BY HELEN EXLEY

Dedicated to Martin Kerr for the awesome creation and design of Helen Exley books, for over two decades. And, especially for the gift of his time to create this book for me during the Covid 19 crisis. Thank you Martin for everything.

Published in 2020 by Helen Exley®LONDON in Great Britain.
All the words by Dalton Exley, Charlotte Gray, Odile Dormeuil, Maya V. Patel, Pamela Dugdale, Hannah C. Klein, Pam Brown and Siân E. Morgan are copyright © Helen Exley Creative Ltd 2020.
Photography by Richard Exley © Helen Exley Creative Ltd 2020.
Design, selection and arrangement by Helen Exley © Helen Exley Creative Ltd 2020.

ISBN 978-1-78485-317-4

12 11 10 9 8 7 6 5 4 3 2 1

Helen Exley®LONDON
16 Chalk Hill, Watford, Hertfordshire, WD19 4BG, UK
www.helenexley.com